my daily prayer

this book belongs to

_____

_____

_____

Date _____   S M T W Th F S

my daily prayer

Today's Scriptures

Lord teach me to.... _____

_____

_____

_____

_____

_____

_____

_____

thank you

I'm praying for ....

prayer requests

_____
_____
_____
_____
_____
_____
_____
_____

reflections

_____
_____
_____
_____
_____
_____
_____
_____

things on my heart

Amen

Date _____   S M T W Th F S

my daily prayer

Today's Scriptures

Lord teach me to.... _____

_____

_____

_____

_____

_____

_____

_____

thank you

I'm praying for ....

prayer requests

_____
_____
_____
_____
_____
_____
_____
_____

reflections

_____
_____
_____
_____
_____
_____
_____
_____
_____
_____

things on my heart

Amen

Date _____   S M T W Th F S

my daily prayer

Today's Scriptures

Lord teach me to.... _____

_____

_____

_____

_____

_____

_____

_____

thank you

I'm praying for ....

prayer requests

_____
_____
_____
_____
_____
_____
_____
_____
_____
_____

reflections

_____
_____
_____
_____
_____
_____
_____
_____
_____
_____

things on my heart

Amen

Date _____   S M T W Th F S

my daily prayer

Today's Scriptures

Lord teach me to.... _____

_____

_____

_____

_____

_____

_____

_____

thank you

I'm praying for ....

prayer requests

_____

_____

_____

_____

_____

_____

_____

reflections

_____

_____

_____

_____

_____

_____

_____

things on my heart

Amen

Date _____   S M T W Th F S

my daily prayer

Today's Scriptures

Lord teach me to.... _____

_____

_____

_____

_____

_____

_____

_____

thank you

I'm praying for ....

prayer requests

_____

_____

_____

_____

_____

_____

_____

reflections

_____

_____

_____

_____

_____

_____

_____

things on my heart

_____

_____

Amen

Date _____   S M T W Th F S

my daily prayer

Today's Scriptures

Lord teach me to.... _____

_____

_____

_____

_____

_____

_____

_____

thank you

I'm praying for ....

prayer requests

_____
_____
_____
_____
_____
_____
_____
_____

reflections

_____
_____
_____
_____
_____
_____
_____
_____

things on my heart

Amen

Date _____   S M T W Th F S

my daily prayer

Today's Scriptures

Lord teach me to.... _____

_____

_____

_____

_____

_____

_____

_____

thank you

I'm praying for ....

prayer requests

_____

_____

_____

_____

_____

_____

_____

reflections

_____

_____

_____

_____

_____

_____

_____

things on my heart

Amen

Date _____   S M T W Th F S

my daily prayer

Today's Scriptures

Lord teach me to.... _____

_____

_____

_____

_____

_____

_____

_____

thank you

I'm praying for ....

prayer requests

_____
_____
_____
_____
_____
_____
_____
_____

reflections

_____
_____
_____
_____
_____
_____
_____
_____

things on my heart

Amen

Date _____   S M T W Th F S

my daily prayer

Today's Scriptures

Lord teach me to.... _____

_____

_____

_____

_____

_____

_____

_____

                                                    thank you

I'm praying for ....

prayer requests

_____
_____
_____
_____
_____
_____
_____
_____

reflections

_____
_____
_____
_____
_____
_____
_____
_____

things on my heart

Amen

Date _____   S M T W Th F S

my daily prayer

Today's Scriptures

Lord teach me to.... _____

_____

_____

_____

_____

_____

_____

_____

thank you

I'm praying for ....

prayer requests

_____
_____
_____
_____
_____
_____
_____
_____

reflections

_____
_____
_____
_____
_____
_____
_____

things on my heart

Amen

Date _____   S M T W Th F S

my daily prayer

Today's Scriptures

Lord teach me to.... _____

_____

_____

_____

_____

_____

_____

_____

thank you

I'm praying for ....

prayer requests

_____

_____

_____

_____

_____

_____

_____

reflections

_____

_____

_____

_____

_____

_____

_____

_____

_____

things on my heart

_____

_____

Amen

Date _____   S M T W Th F S

my daily prayer

Today's Scriptures

Lord teach me to.... _____

_____

_____

_____

_____

_____

_____

_____

thank you

I'm praying for ....

prayer requests

_____
_____
_____
_____
_____
_____
_____
_____
_____
_____

reflections

_____
_____
_____
_____
_____
_____
_____
_____
_____
_____
_____

things on my heart

Amen

Date _____   S M T W Th F S

my daily prayer

Today's Scriptures

Lord teach me to.... _____

_____

_____

_____

_____

_____

_____

_____

                                              thank you

I'm praying for ....

prayer requests

_____
_____
_____
_____
_____
_____
_____
_____

reflections

_____
_____
_____
_____
_____
_____
_____
_____
_____

things on my heart

Amen

Date _____   S M T W Th F S

my daily prayer

Today's Scriptures

Lord teach me to.... _____

_____

_____

_____

_____

_____

_____

_____

thank you

I'm praying for ....

prayer requests

_____
_____
_____
_____
_____
_____
_____
_____

reflections

_____
_____
_____
_____
_____
_____
_____
_____

things on my heart

Amen

Date _____   S M T W Th F S

my daily prayer

Today's Scriptures

Lord teach me to.... _____

_____

_____

_____

_____

_____

_____

_____

thank you

I'm praying for ....

prayer requests

_____
_____
_____
_____
_____
_____
_____
_____
_____

reflections

_____
_____
_____
_____
_____
_____
_____
_____
_____
_____

things on my heart

Amen

Date _____   S M T W Th F S

my daily prayer

Today's Scriptures

Lord teach me to.... _____

_____

_____

_____

_____

_____

_____

thank you

I'm praying for ....

prayer requests

_____
_____
_____
_____
_____
_____
_____

reflections

_____
_____
_____
_____
_____
_____
_____
_____
_____
_____

things on my heart

Amen

Date _____   S M T W Th F S

my daily prayer

Today's Scriptures

Lord teach me to.... _____

_____

_____

_____

_____

_____

_____

_____

                                        thank you

I'm praying for ....

prayer requests

_____
_____
_____
_____
_____
_____
_____
_____
_____

reflections

_____
_____
_____
_____
_____
_____
_____
_____

things on my heart

Amen

Date _____ S M T W Th F S

my daily prayer

Today's Scriptures

Lord teach me to.... _____

_____

_____

_____

_____

_____

_____

_____

thank you

I'm praying for ....

prayer requests

_____
_____
_____
_____
_____
_____
_____
_____

reflections

_____
_____
_____
_____
_____
_____
_____
_____
_____
_____
_____

things on my heart

Amen

Date _____

my daily prayer

Today's Scriptures

Lord teach me to.... _____

_____

_____

_____

_____

_____

_____

_____

thank you

I'm praying for ....

prayer requests

reflections

things on my heart

Amen

Date _____ S M T W Th F S

my daily prayer

Today's Scriptures

Lord teach me to.... _____

_____

_____

_____

_____

_____

_____

thank you

I'm praying for ....

prayer requests

_____
_____
_____
_____
_____
_____
_____
_____
_____

reflections

_____
_____
_____
_____
_____
_____
_____
_____
_____
_____

things on my heart

Amen

Date _____   S M T W Th F S

my daily prayer

Today's Scriptures

Lord teach me to.... _____

_____

_____

_____

_____

_____

_____

_____

thank you

I'm praying for ....

prayer requests

_____
_____
_____
_____
_____
_____
_____
_____
_____
_____

reflections

_____
_____
_____
_____
_____
_____
_____
_____
_____
_____
_____
_____

things on my heart

Amen

Date _____   S M T W Th F S

my daily prayer

Today's Scriptures

Lord teach me to.... _____

_____

_____

_____

_____

_____

_____

thank you

I'm praying for ....

prayer requests

_____
_____
_____
_____
_____
_____
_____
_____
_____
_____
_____

reflections

_____
_____
_____
_____
_____
_____
_____
_____
_____
_____
_____

things on my heart

Amen

Date _____   S M T W Th F S

my daily prayer

Today's Scriptures

Lord teach me to.... _____

_____

_____

_____

_____

_____

_____

_____

thank you

I'm praying for ....

prayer requests

_____

_____

_____

_____

_____

_____

_____

_____

reflections

_____

_____

_____

_____

_____

_____

_____

_____

_____

things on my heart

Amen

Date _____ S M T W Th F S

my daily prayer

Today's Scriptures

Lord teach me to.... _____

_____

_____

_____

_____

_____

_____

_____

thank you

I'm praying for ....

prayer requests

_____
_____
_____
_____
_____
_____
_____
_____

reflections

_____
_____
_____
_____
_____
_____
_____
_____
_____

things on my heart

Amen

Date _____   S M T W Th F S

my daily prayer

Today's Scriptures

Lord teach me to.... _____

_____

_____

_____

_____

_____

_____

_____

thank you

I'm praying for ....

prayer requests

_____

_____

_____

_____

_____

_____

_____

_____

reflections

_____

_____

_____

_____

_____

_____

_____

_____

_____

things on my heart

Amen

Date _____   S M T W Th F S

my daily prayer

Today's Scriptures

Lord teach me to.... _____

_____

_____

_____

_____

_____

_____

_____

                                        thank you

I'm praying for ....

prayer requests

_____
_____
_____
_____
_____
_____
_____
_____

reflections

_____
_____
_____
_____
_____
_____
_____
_____
_____

things on my heart

Amen

Date _____   S M T W Th F S

my daily prayer

Today's Scriptures

Lord teach me to.... _____

_____

_____

_____

_____

_____

_____

thank you

I'm praying for ....

prayer requests

_____
_____
_____
_____
_____
_____
_____
_____
_____

reflections

_____
_____
_____
_____
_____
_____
_____
_____
_____
_____

things on my heart

Amen

Date ＿＿＿＿＿＿＿

my daily prayer

Today's Scriptures

Lord teach me to.... ＿＿＿＿＿＿＿

＿＿＿＿＿＿＿＿＿＿＿＿＿＿＿＿

＿＿＿＿＿＿＿＿＿＿＿＿＿＿＿＿

＿＿＿＿＿＿＿＿＿＿＿＿＿＿＿＿

＿＿＿＿＿＿＿＿＿＿＿＿＿＿＿＿

＿＿＿＿＿＿＿＿＿＿＿＿＿＿＿＿

＿＿＿＿＿＿＿＿＿＿＿＿＿＿＿＿

＿＿＿＿＿＿＿＿＿＿＿＿＿＿＿＿

thank you

I'm praying for ....

prayer requests

_____

_____

_____

_____

_____

_____

_____

reflections

_____

_____

_____

_____

_____

_____

_____

things on my heart

Amen

Date _____   S M T W Th F S

my daily prayer

Today's Scriptures

Lord teach me to.... _____

_____

_____

_____

_____

_____

_____

_____

thank you

I'm praying for ....

prayer requests

_____
_____
_____
_____
_____
_____
_____
_____

reflections

_____
_____
_____
_____
_____
_____
_____
_____

things on my heart

Amen

Date _____

my daily prayer

Today's Scriptures

Lord teach me to.... _____

_____

_____

_____

_____

_____

_____

_____

thank you

I'm praying for ....

prayer requests

_____
_____
_____
_____
_____
_____
_____
_____
_____

reflections

_____
_____
_____
_____
_____
_____
_____
_____
_____
_____

things on my heart

Amen

Date _____ S M T W Th F S

my daily prayer

Today's Scriptures

Lord teach me to.... _____

_____

_____

_____

_____

_____

_____

_____

thank you

I'm praying for ....

prayer requests

_____
_____
_____
_____
_____
_____
_____
_____
_____

reflections

_____
_____
_____
_____
_____
_____
_____
_____

things on my heart

Amen

Date _____   S M T W Th F S

my daily prayer

Today's Scriptures

Lord teach me to.... _____

_____

_____

_____

_____

_____

_____

_____

thank you

I'm praying for ....

prayer requests

_____
_____
_____
_____
_____
_____
_____
_____
_____

reflections

_____
_____
_____
_____
_____
_____
_____
_____
_____
_____

things on my heart

Amen

Date _____ S M T W Th F S

my daily prayer

Today's Scriptures

Lord teach me to.... _____

_____

_____

_____

_____

_____

_____

_____

thank you

I'm praying for ....

prayer requests

_____

_____

_____

_____

_____

_____

_____

_____

reflections

_____

_____

_____

_____

_____

_____

_____

_____

things on my heart

Amen

Date _____   S M T W Th F S

my daily prayer

Today's Scriptures

Lord teach me to.... _____

_____

_____

_____

_____

_____

_____

thank you

I'm praying for ....

prayer requests

_____

_____

_____

_____

_____

_____

_____

_____

reflections

_____

_____

_____

_____

_____

_____

_____

things on my heart

_____

_____

_____

Amen

Date _____   S M T W Th F S

my daily prayer

Today's Scriptures

Lord teach me to.... _____

_____

_____

_____

_____

_____

_____

_____

thank you

I'm praying for ....

prayer requests

_____
_____
_____
_____
_____
_____
_____
_____
_____

reflections

_____
_____
_____
_____
_____
_____
_____
_____
_____
_____
_____

things on my heart

Amen

Date _____ S M T W Th F S

my daily prayer

Today's Scriptures

Lord teach me to.... _____

_____

_____

_____

_____

_____

_____

_____

thank you

I'm praying for ....

prayer requests

_____

_____

_____

_____

_____

_____

_____

_____

reflections

_____

_____

_____

_____

_____

_____

_____

_____

things on my heart

Amen

Date _____   S M T W Th F S

my daily prayer

Today's Scriptures

Lord teach me to.... _____

_____

_____

_____

_____

_____

_____

_____

thank you

I'm praying for ....

prayer requests

_____
_____
_____
_____
_____
_____
_____
_____
_____

reflections

_____
_____
_____
_____
_____
_____
_____
_____

things on my heart

Amen

Date _____

my daily prayer

Today's Scriptures

Lord teach me to.... _____

_____

_____

_____

_____

_____

_____

thank you

I'm praying for ....

prayer requests

_____

_____

_____

_____

_____

_____

_____

_____

reflections

_____

_____

_____

_____

_____

_____

_____

_____

_____

things on my heart

Amen

Date _____   S M T W Th F S

my daily prayer

Today's Scriptures

Lord teach me to.... _____

_____

_____

_____

_____

_____

_____

_____

thank you

I'm praying for ....

prayer requests

reflections

things on my heart

Amen

Date _____ S M T W Th F S

my daily prayer

Today's Scriptures

Lord teach me to.... _____

_____

_____

_____

_____

_____

_____

_____

thank you

I'm praying for ....

prayer requests

_____
_____
_____
_____
_____
_____
_____

reflections

_____
_____
_____
_____
_____
_____
_____
_____
_____
_____

things on my heart

Amen

Date _____

S M T W Th F S

my daily prayer

Today's Scriptures

Lord teach me to.... _____

_____

_____

_____

_____

_____

_____

thank you

I'm praying for ....

prayer requests

_____

_____

_____

_____

_____

_____

_____

_____

reflections

_____

_____

_____

_____

_____

_____

_____

_____

_____

things on my heart

Amen

Date _____   S M T W Th F S

my daily prayer

Today's Scriptures

Lord teach me to.... _____

_____

_____

_____

_____

_____

_____

_____

thank you

I'm praying for ....

prayer requests

_____
_____
_____
_____
_____
_____
_____
_____

reflections

_____
_____
_____
_____
_____
_____
_____
_____
_____

things on my heart

Amen

Date _____   S M T W Th F S

my daily prayer

Today's Scriptures

Lord teach me to.... _____

_____

_____

_____

_____

_____

_____

_____

thank you

I'm praying for ....

prayer requests

_____
_____
_____
_____
_____
_____
_____
_____

reflections

_____
_____
_____
_____
_____
_____
_____
_____

things on my heart

Amen

Date _____ S M T W Th F S

my daily prayer

Today's Scriptures

Lord teach me to.... _____

_____

_____

_____

_____

_____

_____

_____

thank you

I'm praying for ....

prayer requests

_____
_____
_____
_____
_____
_____
_____

reflections

_____
_____
_____
_____
_____
_____
_____
_____
_____

things on my heart

Amen

Date _____   S M T W Th F S

my daily prayer

Today's Scriptures

Lord teach me to.... _____

_____

_____

_____

_____

_____

_____

_____

thank you

I'm praying for ....

prayer requests

reflections

things on my heart

Amen

Date _____   S M T W Th F S

my daily prayer

Today's Scriptures

Lord teach me to.... _____

_____

_____

_____

_____

_____

_____

                                              thank you

I'm praying for ....

prayer requests

_____
_____
_____
_____
_____
_____
_____
_____
_____

reflections

_____
_____
_____
_____
_____
_____
_____
_____
_____
_____

things on my heart

Amen

Date _____   S M T W Th F S

my daily prayer

Today's Scriptures

Lord teach me to.... _____

_____

_____

_____

_____

_____

_____

_____

thank you

I'm praying for ....

prayer requests

_____
_____
_____
_____
_____
_____
_____

reflections

_____
_____
_____
_____
_____
_____
_____
_____
_____
_____

things on my heart

Amen

Date _____   S M T W Th F S

my daily prayer

Today's Scriptures

Lord teach me to.... _____

_____

_____

_____

_____

_____

_____

_____

                                              thank you

I'm praying for ....

prayer requests

_____
_____
_____
_____
_____
_____
_____
_____
_____
_____

reflections

_____
_____
_____
_____
_____
_____
_____
_____
_____
_____
_____

things on my heart

Amen

Date _____   S M T W Th F S

my daily prayer

Today's Scriptures

Lord teach me to.... _____

_____

_____

_____

_____

_____

_____

_____

thank you

I'm praying for ....

prayer requests

_____
_____
_____
_____
_____
_____
_____
_____

reflections

_____
_____
_____
_____
_____
_____
_____
_____

things on my heart

Amen

Date _____   S M T W Th F S

my daily prayer

Today's Scriptures

Lord teach me to.... _____

_____

_____

_____

_____

_____

_____

_____

thank you

I'm praying for ....

prayer requests

_____
_____
_____
_____
_____
_____
_____

reflections

_____
_____
_____
_____
_____
_____
_____
_____

things on my heart

Amen

Date _____ S M T W Th F S

my daily prayer

Today's Scriptures

Lord teach me to.... _____

_____

_____

_____

_____

_____

_____

thank you

I'm praying for ....

prayer requests

_____
_____
_____
_____
_____
_____
_____
_____
_____

reflections

_____
_____
_____
_____
_____
_____
_____
_____
_____
_____
_____
_____

things on my heart

Amen

Date _____   S M T W Th F S

my daily prayer

Today's Scriptures

Lord teach me to.... _____

_____

_____

_____

_____

_____

_____

_____

                                                        thank you

I'm praying for ....

prayer requests

_____
_____
_____
_____
_____
_____
_____
_____

reflections

_____
_____
_____
_____
_____
_____
_____
_____
_____
_____

things on my heart

Amen

Date _____ S M T W Th F S

my daily prayer

Today's Scriptures

Lord teach me to.... _____

_____

_____

_____

_____

_____

_____

_____

thank you

I'm praying for ....

prayer requests

_____
_____
_____
_____
_____
_____
_____
_____
_____

reflections

_____
_____
_____
_____
_____
_____
_____

things on my heart

_____
_____

Amen

Date _____   S M T W Th F S

my daily prayer

Today's Scriptures

Lord teach me to.... _____

_____

_____

_____

_____

_____

_____

_____

thank you

I'm praying for ....

prayer requests

_____
_____
_____
_____
_____
_____
_____
_____
_____
_____

reflections

_____
_____
_____
_____
_____
_____
_____
_____
_____

things on my heart

Amen

Date _____   S M T W Th F S

my daily prayer

Today's Scriptures

Lord teach me to.... _____

_____

_____

_____

_____

_____

_____

_____

thank you

I'm praying for ....

prayer requests

_____
_____
_____
_____
_____
_____
_____
_____

reflections

_____
_____
_____
_____
_____
_____
_____

things on my heart

Amen

Date _____

my daily prayer

Today's Scriptures

Lord teach me to.... _____

_____

_____

_____

_____

_____

_____

_____

thank you

I'm praying for ....

prayer requests

_____

_____

_____

_____

_____

_____

_____

_____

reflections

_____

_____

_____

_____

_____

_____

_____

_____

_____

things on my heart

Amen

Date _____   S M T W Th F S

my daily prayer

Today's Scriptures

Lord teach me to.... _____

_____

_____

_____

_____

_____

_____

_____

thank you

I'm praying for ....

prayer requests

---

reflections

---

things on my heart

Amen

Date _____ S M T W Th F S

my daily prayer

Today's Scriptures

Lord teach me to.... _____

_____

_____

_____

_____

_____

_____

thank you

I'm praying for ....

prayer requests

_____
_____
_____
_____
_____
_____
_____
_____

reflections

_____
_____
_____
_____
_____
_____
_____
_____
_____

things on my heart

Amen

Date _____   S M T W Th F S

my daily prayer

Today's Scriptures

Lord teach me to.... _____

_____

_____

_____

_____

_____

_____

_____

thank you

I'm praying for ....

prayer requests

_____

_____

_____

_____

_____

_____

_____

reflections

_____

_____

_____

_____

_____

_____

_____

things on my heart

Amen

Thank You!

my daily prayer

so much for trying our Dailey Prayer Notebook!
We'd love to hear from you!

If you've found this to be a good book please,
support us and leave a review.

If you have any suggestions or issues with this book, or if
you want to test some of our latest notebooks
please email us.

Send email to:

pickme.readme@gmail.com

www.ingramcontent.com/pod-product-compliance
Lightning Source LLC
Chambersburg PA
CBHW071202120626
46546CB00006B/2386